Celebrated Piano Solos

Eight Diverse Solos for Early Intermediate to Intermediate Pianists

(UK Exam Grades 2 & 3)

Robert D. Vandall

I always appreciate a supplemental solo book that provides musical variety for my students. These solos, many of which have been chosen for local and national festivals, represent many different styles, moods, keys, meter signatures, tempos, and pianistic techniques. Skip around in this collection and follow your students' interests, celebrating the diversity of their musical tastes and the variety this collection provides for them!

Robert D. Vandall

Contents

Alfred

On the Lake

(Barcarolle)

Robert D. Vandall

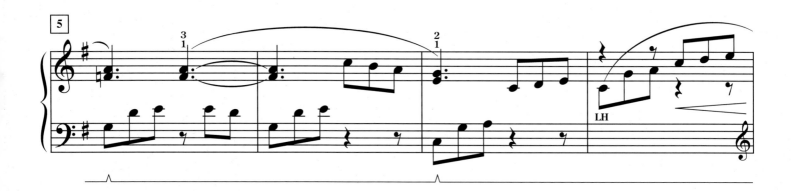

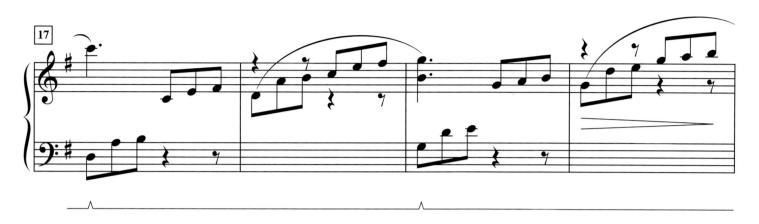

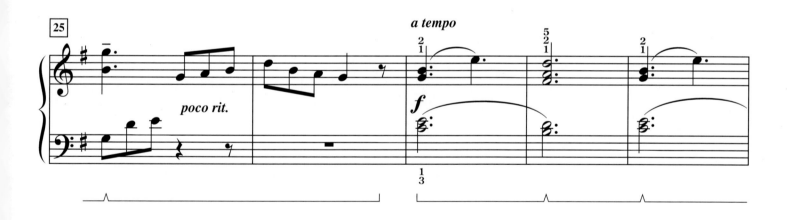

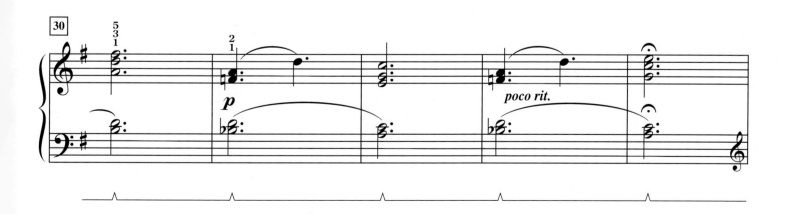

4

5

Imagination

Robert D. Vandall

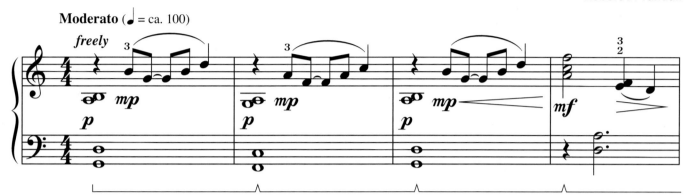

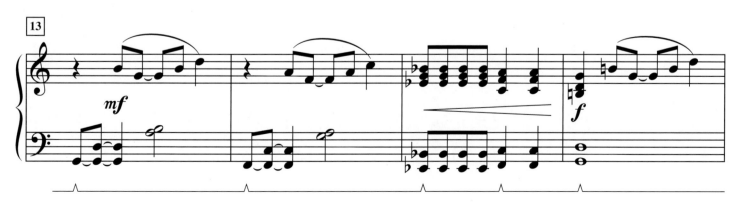

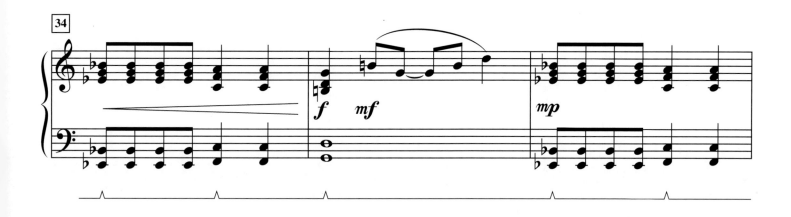

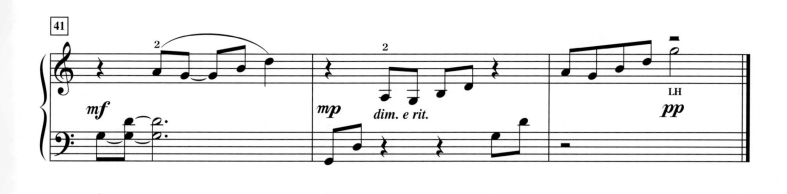

Sugar Valley Reel

Robert D. Vandall

Light Syncopations

Robert D. Vandall

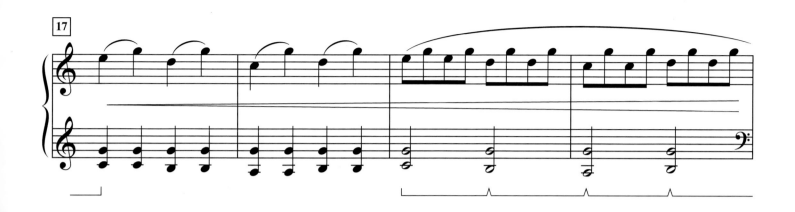

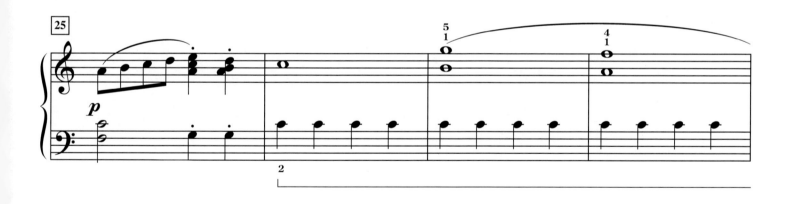

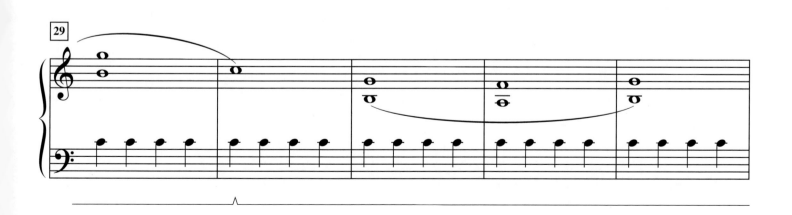

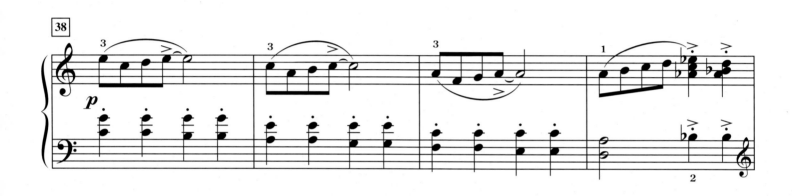

Swing It!

Robert D. Vandall

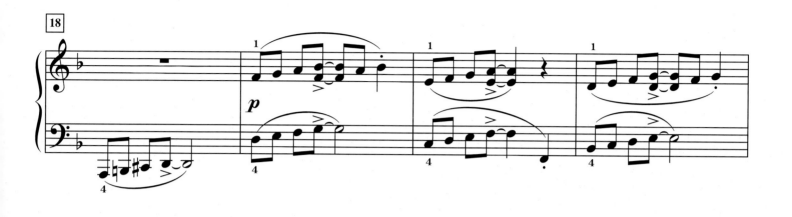

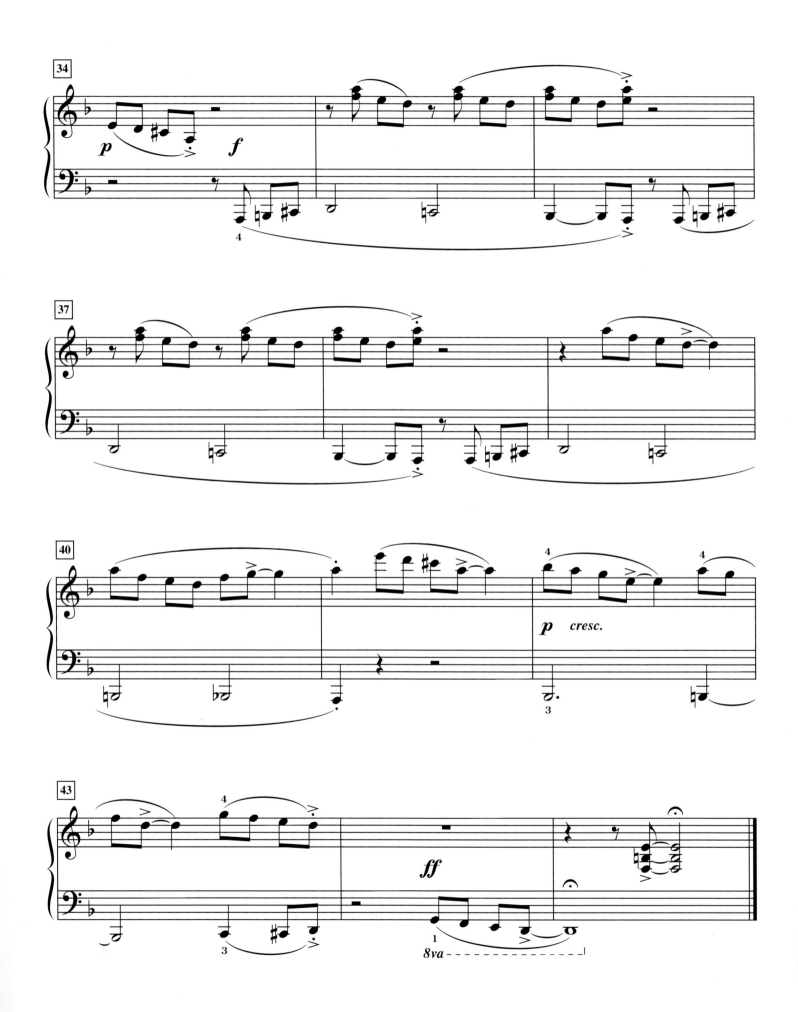

Daydream

Robert D. Vandall

Cloudy Day

Robert D. Vandall

Propulsion

Robert D. Vandall

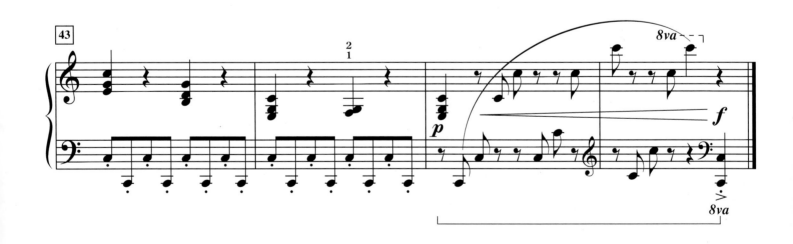